MATHS ...US ...N

USIN... ...BULARY

Maths Language Activities

for 5–7 year olds

David Kirkby

Heinemann

Heinemann
Halley Court, Jordan Hill, Oxford, OX2 8EJ
a division of Reed Educational and Professional Publishing Ltd
www.heinemann.co.uk

Heinemann is a registered trademark of Reed Educational and Professional Publishing Ltd

First published 2001

06 05 04 03 02 01
10 9 8 7 6 5 4 3 2 1

ISBN 0435 186736

Designed by Jonathan Williams
Illustrated by Simone Abel, Oxford Illustrators and Jonathan Williams

Printed and bound by Page Bros (Norwich) Ltd

Contents

	Page
Introduction	**4**
Using the Dictionary and Maths Language Activities	**4**
Dictionary games	**5**
Vocabulary activities and displays	**7**
'Show me' activities	**8**
Copymaster activities	**9**
Copymasters (1-44)	**10-32**

Numbers and the number system

1 even number
2 odd number
3 sequence
4 estimate
5 more, less
6 half, quarter

Calculations

7 add, plus
8 total
9 subtract
10 difference
11 double
12 double, half
13 times table
14 multiply
15 divide by 2
16 divide by 5

Solving problems

17 coin
18 change
19 block graph
20 pictogram

Measures

21 longer, longest
22 shorter, shortest
23 taller, tallest
24 estimate, centimetre
25 half past
26 quarter past
27 quarter to
28 month
29 day
30 today, tomorrow, yesterday
31 time words (second, minute, hour, day, week, month, year)

Shape and space

32 edge, face, corner
33 side
34 corner
35 circle
36 triangle
37 square
38 rectangle
39 pentagon
40 hexagon
41 flat shape names (square, triangle, rectangle, circle, pentagon, hexagon, octagon)
42 solid shape names (cube, cuboid, pyramid, cone, cylinder, sphere)
43 symmetry
44 right-angle

Introduction

The *Maths Language Activities* and the *Dictionary* jointly provide a resource to support the development of children's mathematics vocabulary at Key Stage 1. Since the use of the *Dictionary* is dependent on a child's reading skills, this resource is likely to be more appropriate at Year 2. Nevertheless, some of the Copymasters and activities described in this book will be suitable for Year 1 children.

The words included in the *Dictionary* are a selection of the more 'mathematical words' contained in the National Numeracy Strategy *Mathematical Vocabulary* lists. Some instructional or positional words have therefore been excluded. The words included within the Copymasters are a selection of the key words from the *Dictionary*.

The *Dictionary* has been written specifically for 5 to 7 year olds. The definitions are supported by lively colour cartoons and diagrams to aid understanding. Features include an A-Z finger index down the side of each page to help children find the right page.

Words related to each definition in the *Dictionary* are included in bold type, either within the definition itself or by ***See also*** at the beginning of the definition.

half, halve **See also: half past, half turn**

Each of these is a **half**.
A half is a **fraction**.
There are two halves
in a whole.

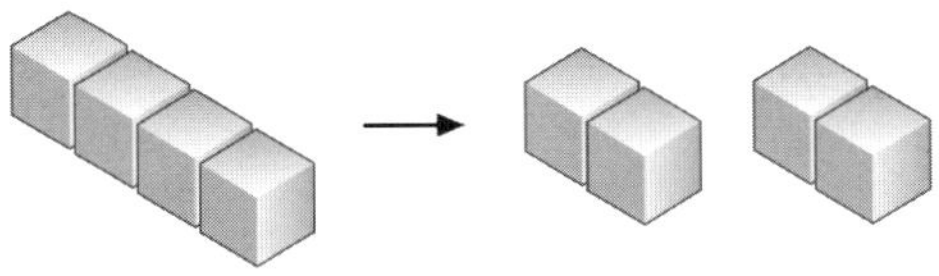

When you **halve** something,
you **divide** it into two equal parts.

Using the Dictionary and Maths Language Activities

The *Maths Language Activities* are of two types. The first part of this book contains teaching activities to help the children become familiar with the *Dictionary*, and to consolidate their knowledge of maths vocabulary. These can be used either at the start of a lesson or topic to introduce new words to the children, or at the end of a lesson or topic to consolidate and assess the children's learning. The second part consists of 44 Copymasters which can be used to reinforce the children's understanding of a new or revised word.

Meeting a new word in class

The *Dictionary* can be used when the children are introduced to a new word. Describe the word to the children and give an illustration of how it is used in a mathematical context. The children can then check the reference in the *Dictionary* before consolidating their understanding of the new word by completing a related Copymaster from the *Maths Language Activities*.

Rehearsing words already met

The *Dictionary* can also be used when the children are rehearsing a word that they have already met, for example a word from the 'vocabulary wall' in their classroom. In this instance you and the children should check the reference in the *Dictionary* before completing a follow-up activity or Copymaster.

Dictionary games

These activities will help children to become familiar with the *Dictionary*, and to consolidate their knowledge of maths vocabulary. They should also help to consolidate children's dictionary skills.

For many of these activities it will be useful to create a bank of 'vocabulary cards'. These can also be used to highlight the key words relating to a lesson or unit of work.

* Find the word

Select a vocabulary card. — Hold it up.

Recognise the word. — Say it together.

Check understanding. — Who can say what it means?

Use the *Dictionary*. — Find it in your *Dictionary*.

Use the word. — Who can use the word in a sentence?

* Guess the word

Photocopy a definition from the *Dictionary* onto an OHT. — Show the OHT to the class, but cover up the word each time it occurs.

Use the *Dictionary*. — Can you find the word?

Check results. — Reveal the hidden word.

Consolidate the meaning. — Discuss it together.

* Name the shape

Choose a shape. — Hold up the shape.

Use the *Dictionary*. — Find the word to match this shape.

Consolidate its properties. — Read the description together.

Recognise the shape. — Can you see the shape in this room?

* Dictionary detectives

Open the *Dictionary* and select a word.	I am looking at a page in the *Dictionary*.
Give a description.	My word means . . . e.g. 'They are not even numbers.' e.g. 'It is a shape with five sides.'
Use the *Dictionary*.	Can you find my page?
Consolidate the meaning.	Read the description together.

* Solve the clues

Select a word.	I am thinking of a word in the *Dictionary*.
Give a clue to its first letter **or** page.	It begins with 'c'. **or** It is on page 7 or 8.
Give further clues.	It has four letters. It is a solid shape.
Consolidate the meaning.	Read the description together.
Use the word.	Who can use this word in a sentence?

* How many?

Select a letter.	The letter is 'c'.
Focus on words which begin with the letter.	Can you think of four words that begin with 'c'?
Use the *Dictionary*.	How many words can you find beginning with 'c'?
Check the counting.	How many words did you find? Does everyone agree?

*Word chains

Select the words.	Hold up a word that has 'See also' words in its definition.
Read the 'See also' words.	Say the words to your maths partner.
Use the *Dictionary*.	Find each word in turn and read what it says.
Consolidate the meaning.	Say a sentence that uses two of the words.

Vocabulary activities and displays

* Vocabulary walls

Create a 'maths vocabulary' wall in your classroom. You can develop this throughout the year or term, and update it as new words are introduced. The vocabulary cards should be stuck onto the wall. The children can then draw pictures or write their own descriptions to define the words. The words could be grouped, for example: 'half' and 'quarter'; 'even number', and 'odd number'.

Vocabulary walls can also be created for specific maths topics. For example, 'A shape vocabulary wall', 'A measures vocabulary wall', 'A numbers vocabulary wall'.

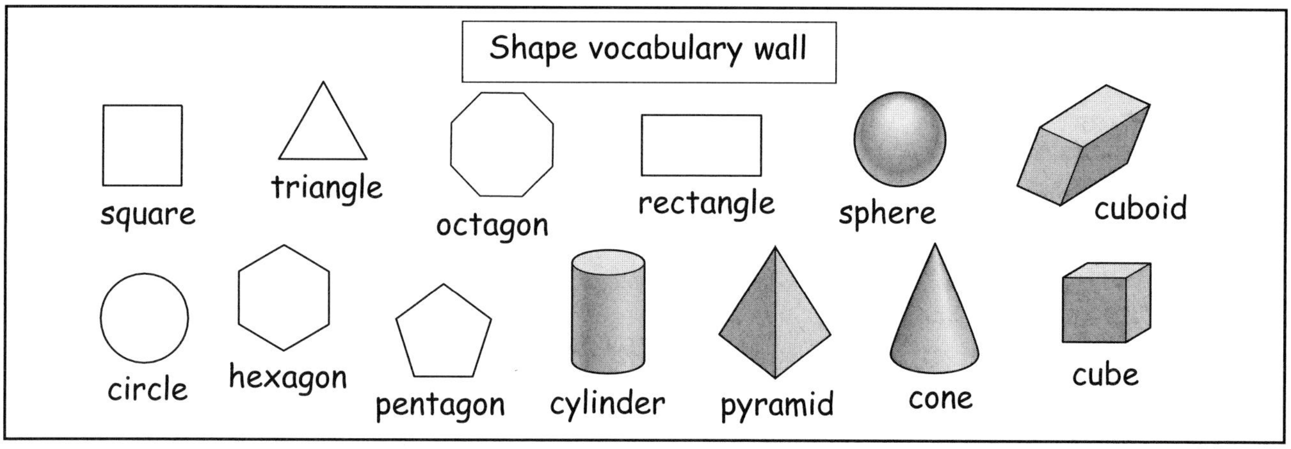

Alternatively, groups of children could make posters to explain maths vocabulary for specific maths topics.

* 'A to Z' of maths vocabulary

Create a frieze around the wall, labelled 'a', 'b', 'c', ..., 'z'. As words are met, attach the matching vocabulary card to the frieze underneath its first letter. This serves as a record of words met throughout the year, and as a resource to support the memory of words and their meaning.

* Word of the week

Choose a different word each week, such as, 'cube'. This becomes a key word for the week. Children can be challenged to say it, to write it, to describe it, to draw it, to build one, to see one, to find it in the *Dictionary*, and so on.

* Concept mapping

Ask the children to suggest words related to a maths topic or supply words you want them to be able to use. Ask the children to use any two words in one sentence. For example:

Topic	money
Words	coin, pence, pounds, note, cost, paid, change
Sentence	'Five one pound coins are worth the same as a five pound note.'

To display, write the words on cards and stick them on the board. Draw a line between the two words used and write the sentence on the line. This activity can be used to assess children's knowledge at the beginning or end of a topic, if individual children's responses are recorded.

* Missing number descriptions

Use a number washing line. Remove a number from the line, for example, 5.

Explain to the children that:

> *A number has gone missing overnight, so we need to ring up the police to give a description of the number. We have to describe the number, but we can't say its name.*

Invite the children to give descriptions. For example:

> *It is made of curved and straight lines.*
> *It is more than 4, more than 2, more than 3,...*
> *It is less than 6, less than 8, less than 9,...*
> *It is between 4 and 6, between 3 and 10,...*
> *It is an odd number.*
> *It is the number of toes on my foot.*
> *It is the number of sides of a pentagon.*

* Using a telephone

The children should use toy or imaginary telephones, in pairs. For example, one child is in charge of the 'Shape shop' and has a collection of shapes. The other child telephones the shape shop and orders a shape by describing it, but not naming it. The activity can be extended to a 'Number shop', a 'Money shop', and so on.

'Show me' activities

The first part of each mathematics lesson normally focuses on developing children's oral work and mental skills. This helps children to practise hearing and using mathematical vocabulary, and is a good time to introduce or rehearse the use of particular words. 'Show me' activities of the type illustrated below and on the next page provide a versatile way of doing this. They can also be used for assessment purposes, particularly if you have an adult helper in the classroom who can observe the responses of two or three children.

For the following activities each child will need a set of 0 to 9 number cards.

* Addition and Subtraction

Show me: *three **add** two...three **more than** two...*
*three **plus** two...the **total** of three and two...*

*five **take away** two...five **subtract** two...*
*two **less than** five...five **minus** two...*
*the **difference** between two and five.*

* Multiplication and division

Show me: *four **twos**… four **lots of** two…*
*four **times** two… our **multiplied by** two…*
*a **multiple** of two…*

*eight **divided by** two… eight **shared between** two…*
*eight **shared by** two… **how many twos** make eight…*

***double** three… **half** of eight… **twice** six… , etc*

* Number

Show me: *a number **more than** five… a number **less than** six…*
*a number **between** seven and ten… an **odd number** more than seven…*
*an **even number** less than eight… a **three-digit number**…*
*the next number in this **sequence:** two four, six…*

For the following activity children should work in pairs. Each pair will need a set of 2D and 3D shapes.

* Shape

Show me: *a **rectangle***
*a **flat** shape with five **sides***
*a **flat** shape with three **corners***

*a **cube***
*a **solid** shape with a **curved face***
*a **solid** shape with **flat faces***
*a **solid** shape with a **square face***
*a **solid** shape with a **curved edge***
*a **solid** shape with a **circular face**.*

Copymaster activities

The Copymasters which follow can be used to consolidate or assess children's understanding of new or revised words. Each Copymaster can be cut in half so that one word can be reinforced or assessed at a time. The Copymasters also have dashed lines alongside each key word so that children can practise writing the word.

The Copymasters are organised by topic: numbers and the number system, calculations, solving problems, measures and shape and space.

Name: ....

1

even number _ _ _ _ _ _ _ _ _ _ _ _ _

Colour the **even numbers** blue.

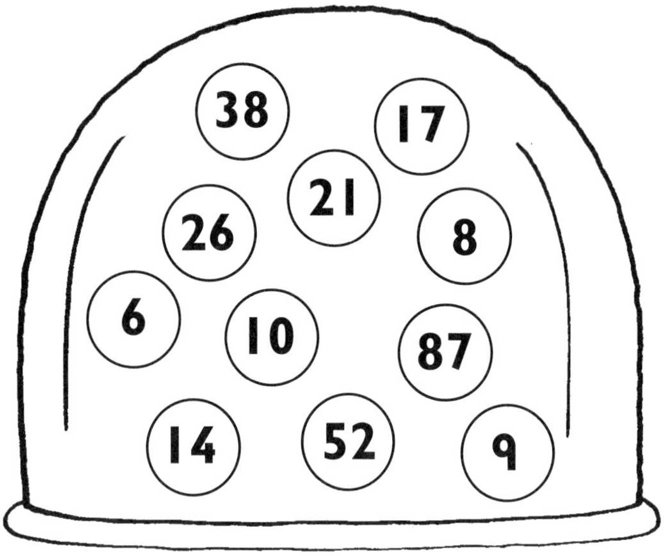

Write six more **even numbers**.

Name: ....

2

odd number _ _ _ _ _ _ _ _ _ _ _

Colour the **odd numbers** green.

1	2	3	4	5	6
7	8	9	10	11	12
13	14	15	16	17	18
19	20	21	22	23	24
25	26	27	28	29	30

Write six more **odd numbers**.

Name: ....

3

sequence ___ ___ ___ ___ ___ ___ ___

Write the next three numbers in each **sequence**.

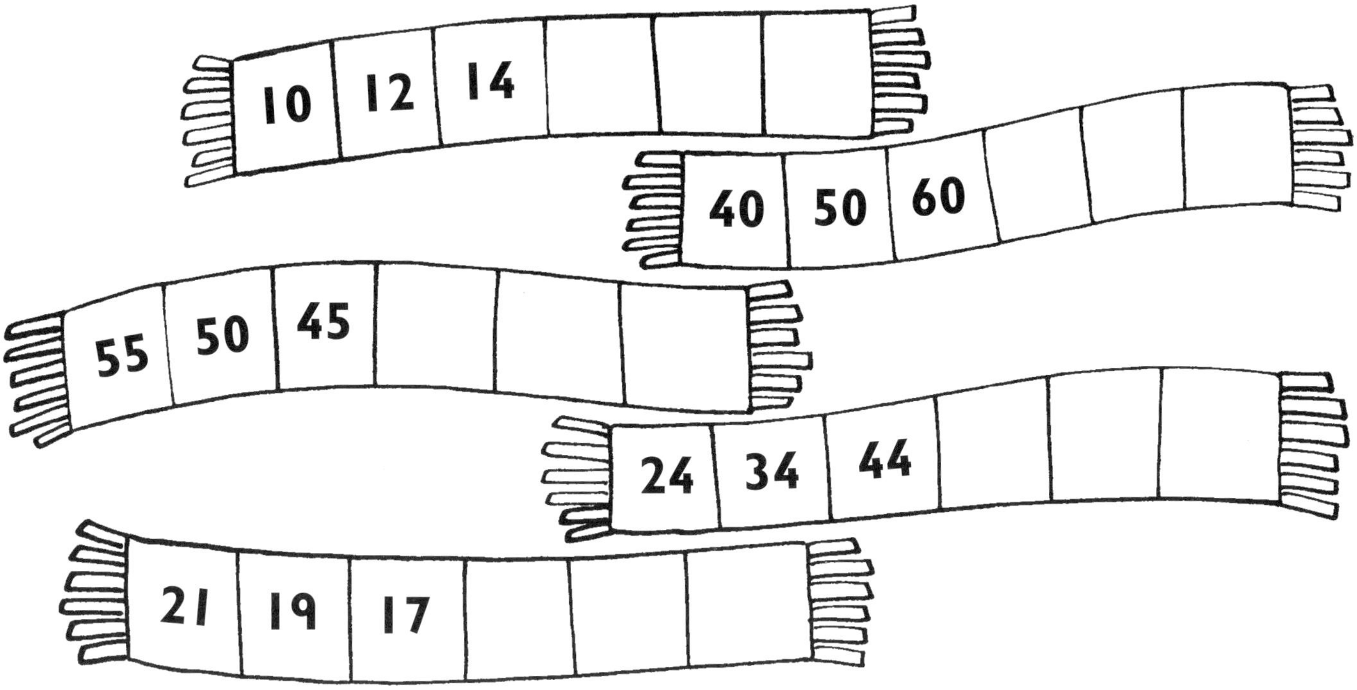

Name: ....

4

estimate ___ ___ ___ ___ ___ ___ ___

Choose and colour one of the three **estimates**.

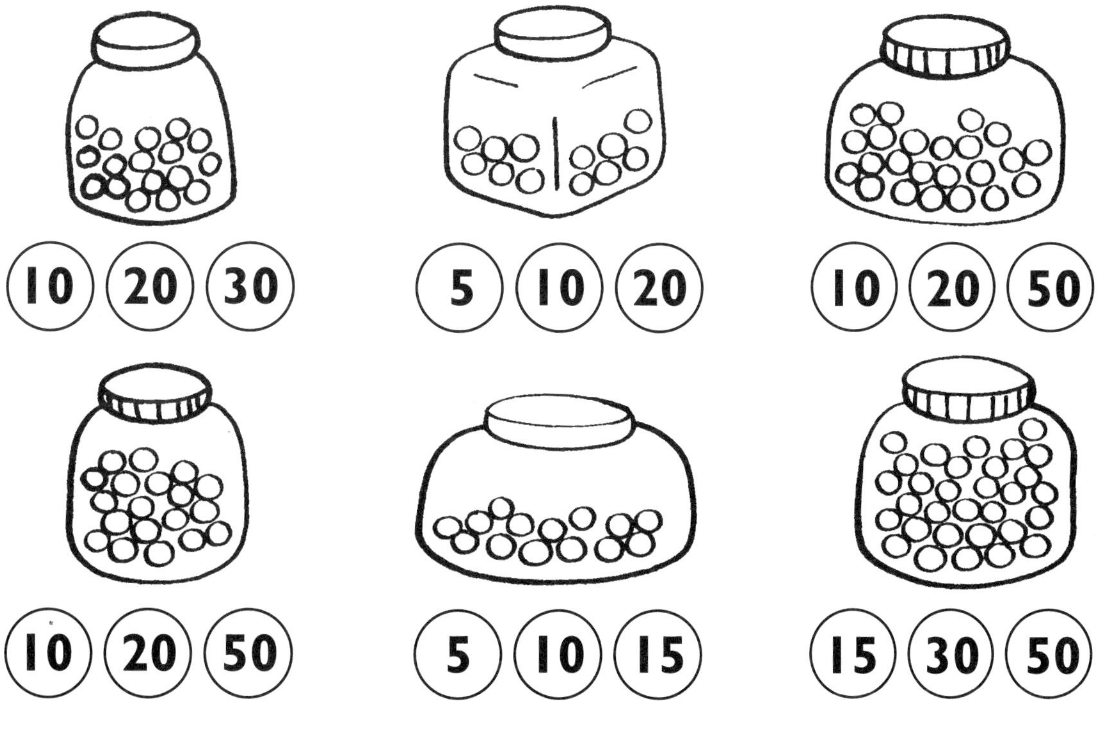

Name: **5**

more _ _ _ _ **less** _ _ _ _

Complete.

12	1 more →	☐	16	1 less →	☐
9	1 more →	☐	35	1 less →	☐
☐	1 more →	17	☐	1 less →	23
36	10 more →	☐	27	10 less →	☐
18	2 more →	☐	41	2 less →	☐

Name: **6**

half _ _ _ _ **quarter** _ _ _ _ _ _ _

Write '**half**' or '**quarter**' for each shaded part.

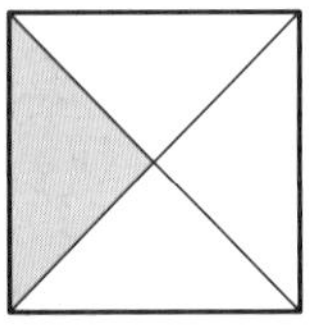

____

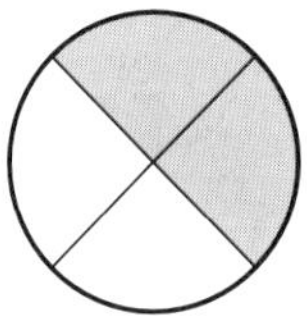

____

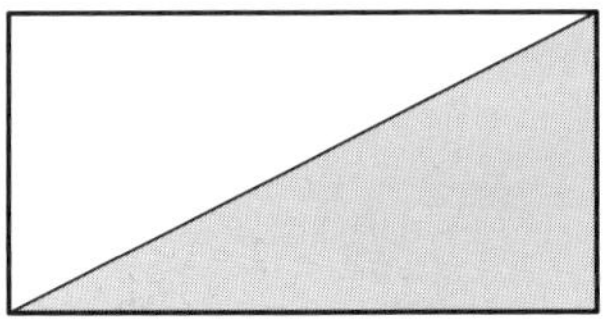

____

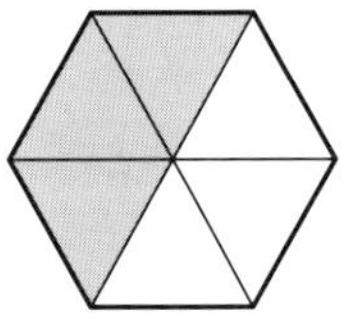

____

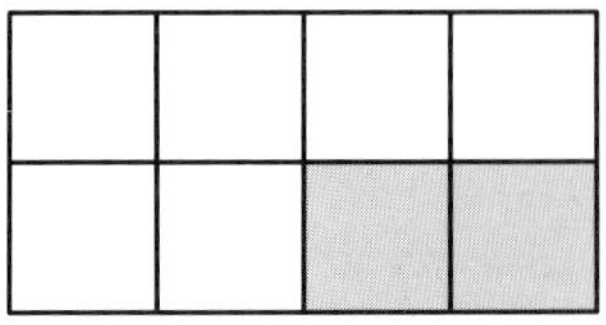

____

Name: **7**

add _ _ _ **plus** _ _ _ _

Complete.

5 + 3 = ☐ 11 + 4 = ☐

28 + 5 = ☐ 30 + 40 = ☐

15 add 6 = ☐ 37 add 11 = ☐

27 plus ☐ = 34 9 plus ☐ = 16

31 + ☐ = 40 ☐ + 40 = 100

Name: **8**

total _ _ _ _ _

Write the **total** of each amount.

total ☐ p

total ☐ p

total ☐ p

Write a pair of numbers for each **total**.

☐ ☐ total **7**

☐ ☐ total **11**

☐ ☐ total **100**

Name: ....

9

subtract __ __ __ __ __ __ __ __

Complete.

6 – 2 = ☐ 13 – 7 = ☐

9 – 4 = ☐ 20 – 5 = ☐

7 take away 3 = ☐ 9 subtract 3 = ☐

10 subtract ☐ = 3 20 subtract 11 = ☐

26 – ☐ = 19 ☐ – 5 = 13

Name: ....

10

difference __ __ __ __ __ __ __ __ __ __

Write the **difference** between each pair.

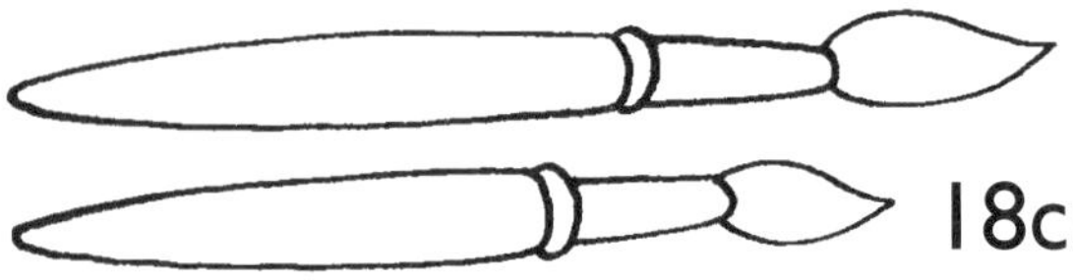

22cm

18cm

difference = ☐ cm

difference = ☐

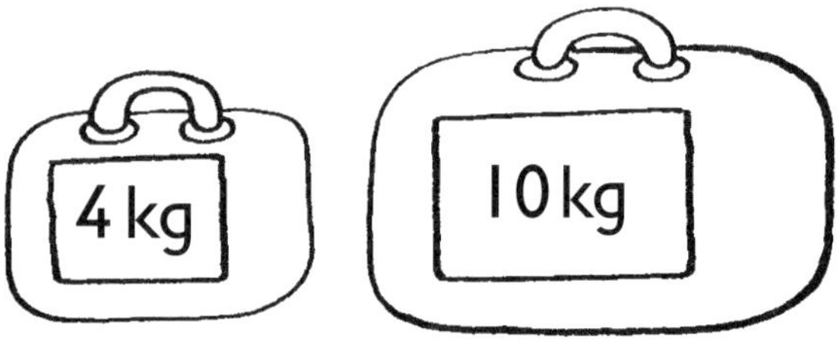

difference = ☐ kg

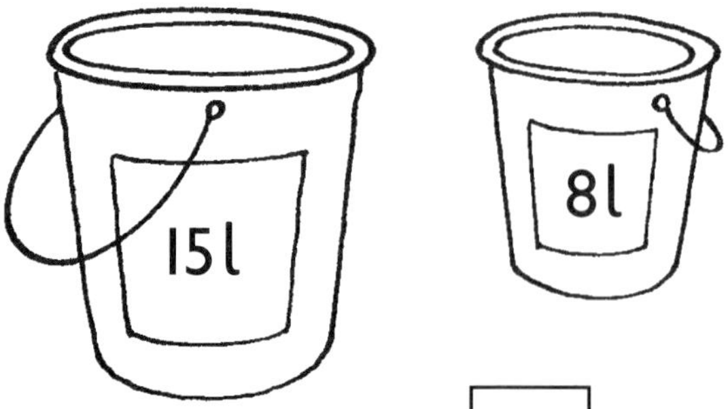

difference = ☐ l

Name: 11

double _ _ _ _ _ _

double 4 is ☐

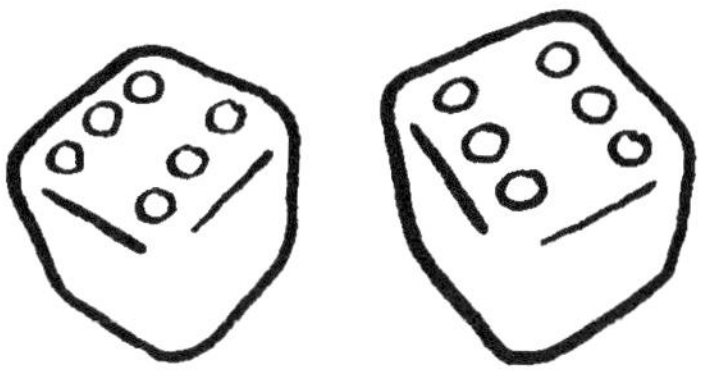

double 6 is ☐

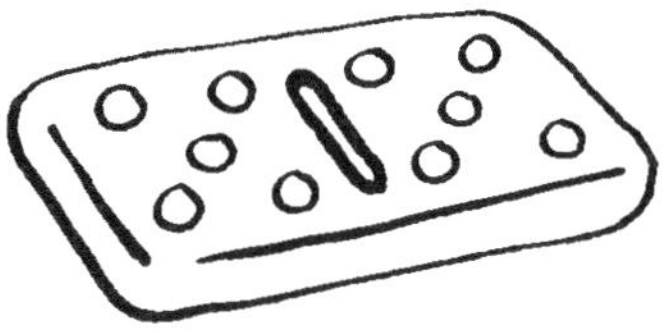

double 5 is ☐

Join each number to its **double**.

(3) (4) (9)

[8] [18] [6]

- -

Name: 12

double _ _ _ _ _ _ **half** _ _ _ _

half of 16 is ☐

half of ☐ is 9

double 6 is ☐

14 is **double** ☐

11 is **half** of ☐

double ☐ is 8

14 is ______________ 7

10 is ______________ 20

Name: **13**

times table __ __ __ __ __   __ __ __ __ __

Complete the **times tables**.

× 2 table
- 1 × 2 = 2
- 2 × 2 =
- 3 × 2 =
- 4 × 2 =
- 5 × 2 = 10
- 6 × 2 =
- 7 × 2 =
- 8 × 2 = 16
- 9 × 2 =
- 10 × 2 =

× 10 table
- 1 × 10 = 10
- 2 × 10 =
- 3 × 10 =
- 4 × 10 = 40
- 5 × 10 =
- 6 × 10 =
- 7 × 10 =
- 8 × 10 =
- 9 × 10 = 90
- 10 × 10 =

× 5 table
- 1 × 5 = 5
- 2 × 5 =
- 3 × 5 = 15
- 4 × 5 =
- 5 × 5 =
- 6 × 5 = 30
- 7 × 5 =
- 8 × 5 =
- 9 × 5 =
- 10 × 5 =

Name: **14**

multiply __ __ __ __ __ __ __ __

Multiply the rows and columns in each set.

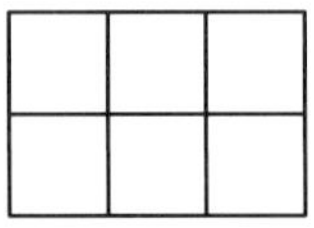

2 x 3 = 6

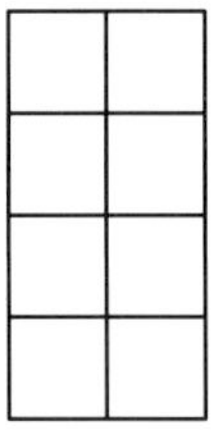

__ x __ = __

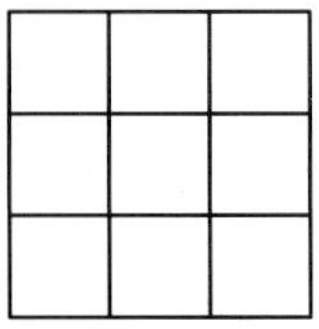

__ x __ = __

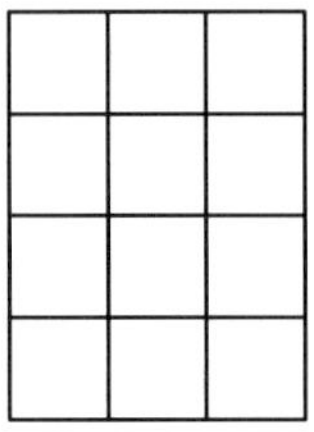

__ x __ = __

__ x __ = __

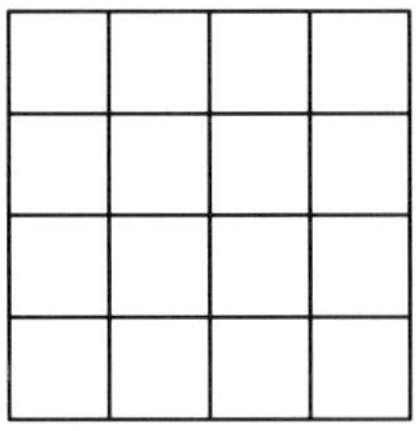

__ x __ = __

Name: ....

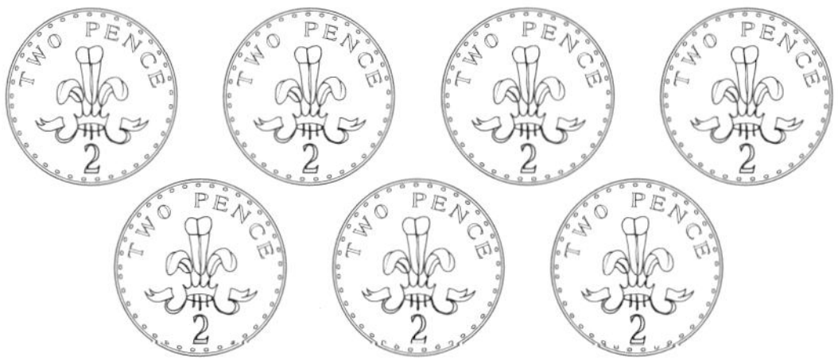

divide by 2 _ _ _ _ _ _ _ _

Write how many 2p coins you need for each item.

☐ 2p coins

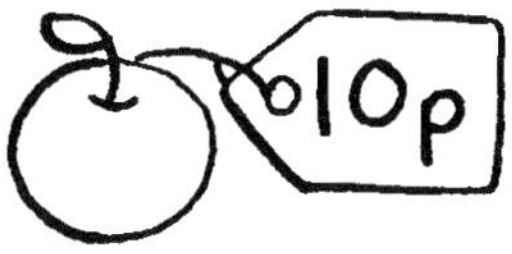

☐ 2p coins

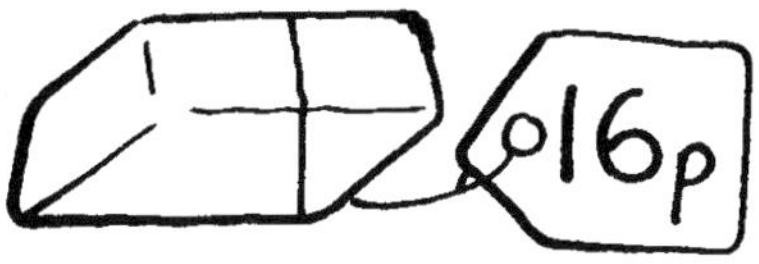

☐ 2p coins

☐ 2p coins

☐ 2p coins

☐ 2p coins

Name: ....

divide by 5 _ _ _ _ _ _ _ _

Write how many 5p stamps you can buy with each amount.

☐ stamps

☐ stamps

☐ stamps

☐ stamps

☐ stamps

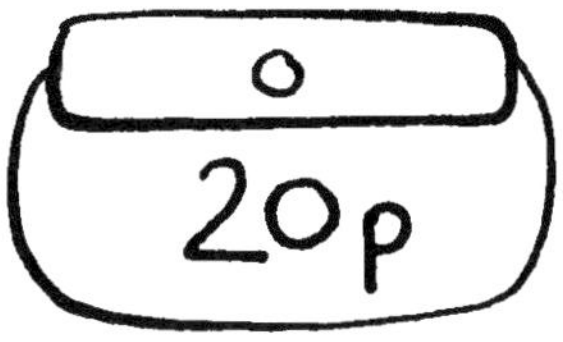

☐ stamps

Name: ....

coin _ _ _ _

Colour the fewest **coins** you need to make each amount.

Write how many **coins** you colour.

23p

☐ coins

38p

☐ coins

56p

☐ coins

Name: ....

change _ _ _ _ _ _

Write how much **change**.

price	pay	change
price 16p		______
price 6p		______
price 45p		______
price 35p		______
price 12p		______
price 28p		______

Name: ....

19

block graph _ _ _ _ _   _ _ _ _ _

How many people like:

plums? ☐

bananas? ☐

pears? ☐

apples? ☐

plums or pears? ☐

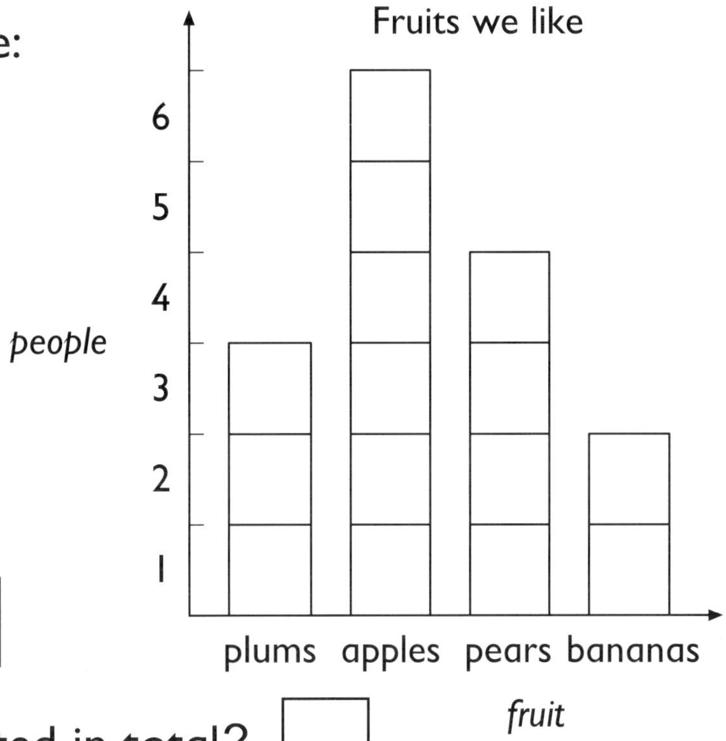

How many people voted in total? ☐

Name: ....

20

pictogram _ _ _ _ _ _ _ _ _

How many sunny days in:

April? ☐

June? ☐

May? ☐

March? ☐

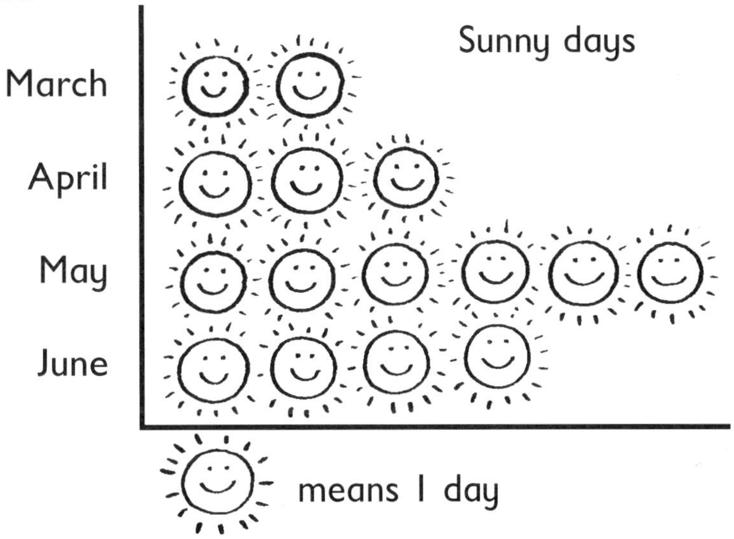

How many more in:

May than June? ☐

June than March? ☐

Name: ....

21

longer _ _ _ _ _ _

longest _ _ _ _ _ _ _

Draw a **longer** bat.

Colour the **longest** bat yellow.

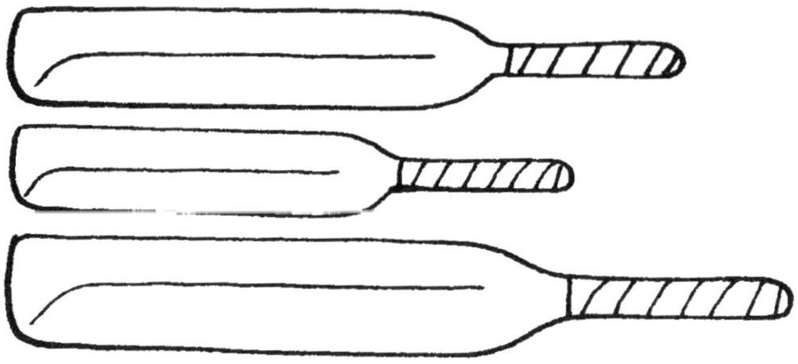

- - - - - - - - - - - - - - - - - - - -

Name: ....

22

shorter _ _ _ _ _ _ _

shortest _ _ _ _ _ _ _ _

Draw a **shorter** pencil.

Colour the **shortest** pen red.

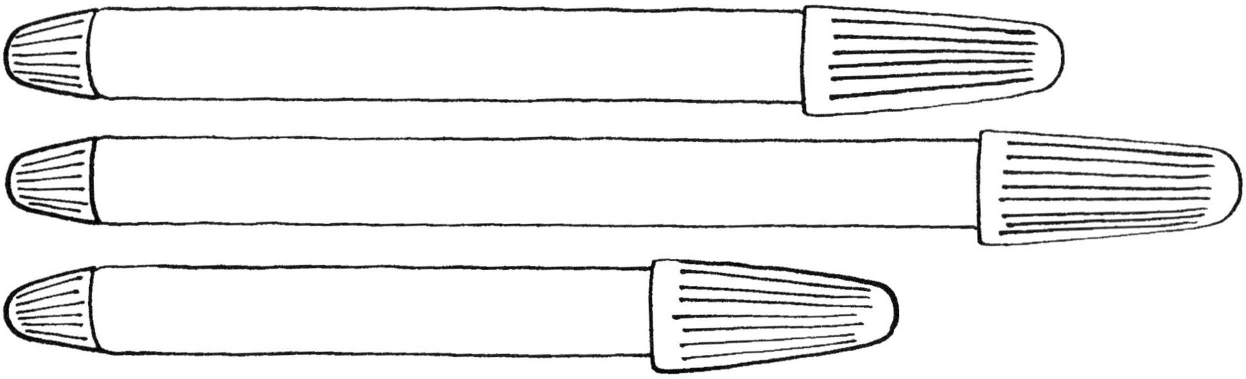

Name: **23**

taller _ _ _ _ _ _ _ , **tallest** _ _ _ _ _ _ _ _

Draw a **taller** tree.

Colour the **tallest** giraffe yellow.

Name: **24**

estimate _ _ _ _ _ _ _ _

centimetre _ _ _ _ _ _ _ _ _ _

Estimate, then measure the length of each straw in **centimetres**.

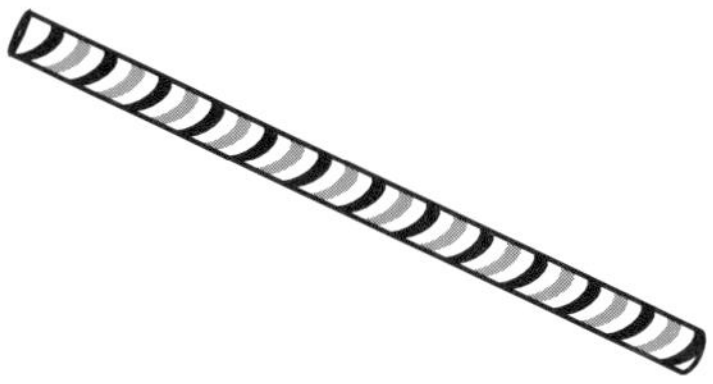

estimate ____ **centimetres** **estimate** ____ **centimetres**

measure ____ **centimetres** measure ____ **centimetres**

half past _ _ _ _   _ _ _ _

Write the times.

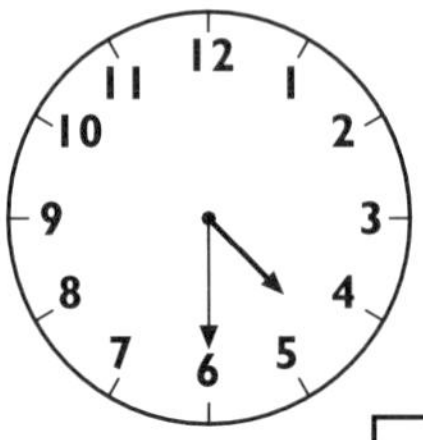

half past ☐

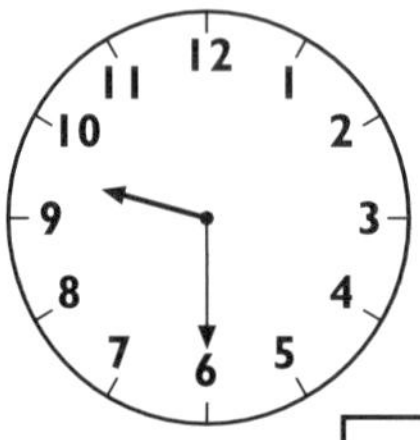

half past ☐

7:30

half past ☐

Show these times on the clocks.

half past 2

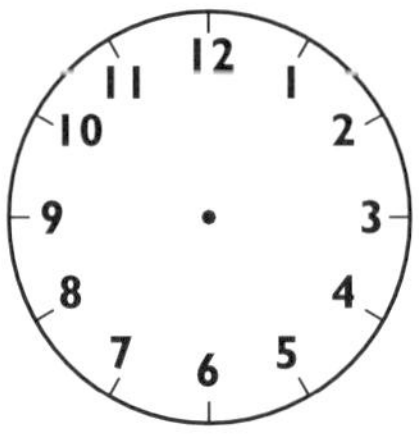

half past 10

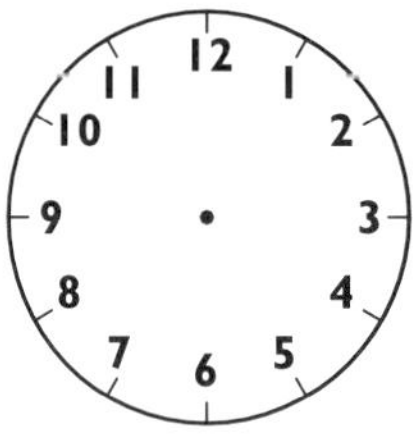

half past 5

:

quarter past _ _ _ _ _ _ _   _ _ _ _

Write the times.

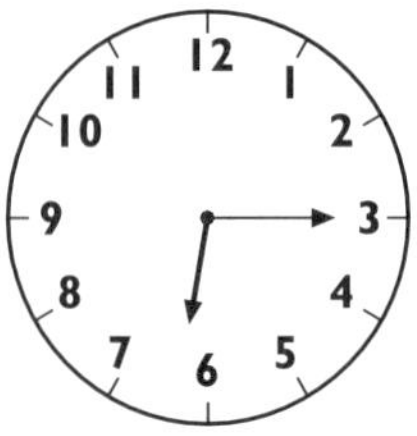

quarter past ☐

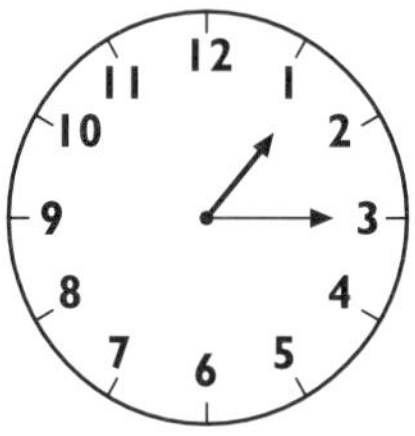

quarter past ☐

8:15

quarter past ☐

Show these times on the clocks.

quarter past 7

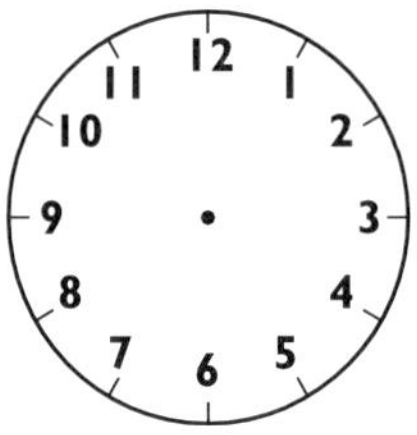

quarter past 9

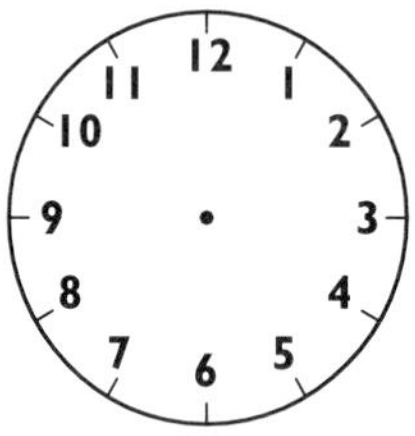

quarter past 4

:

Name: ....

quarter to _ _ _ _ _ _ _ _ _   _ _

Write the times.

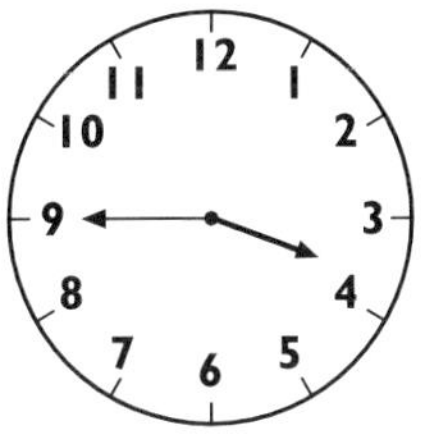

quarter to ☐

quarter to ☐

4:45

quarter to ☐

Show these times on the clocks.

quarter to 6

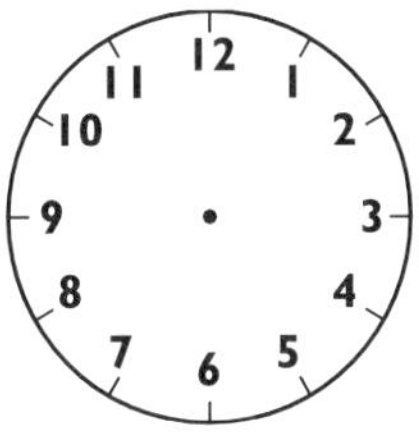

quarter to 11

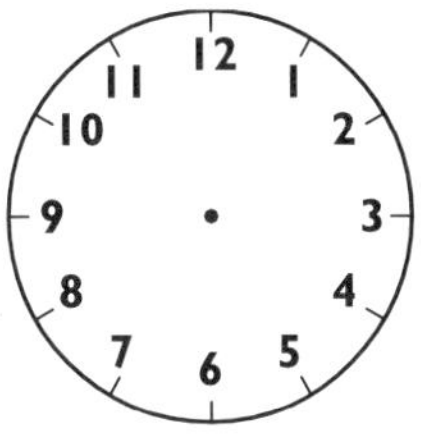

quarter to 7

:

Name: ....

month _ _ _ _ _

Write the **months** in order.

May April March June

__________ __________ __________ __________

September July October August

__________ __________ __________ __________

Name: ....

day _ _ _

Write the missing **days**.

Wednesday,	__________,	Friday
Saturday,	__________,	Monday

Thursday,	Friday,	__________,
__________,	Monday,	Tuesday

Name: ....

today _ _ _ _ _

tomorrow _ _ _ _ _ _ _ _ _

yesterday _ _ _ _ _ _ _ _ _

Write the missing day.

today	Monday
tomorrow	__________

today	Saturday
tomorrow	__________

yesterday	Friday
today	__________

yesterday	Tuesday
today	__________

Name: ....

time words

Write each of these amounts of time in order of length.

Start with the shortest.

hour **year** **second** **week**

minute **month** **day**

______ ______ ______ ______

______ ______ ______

Name: ....

edge _ _ _ _ **face** _ _ _ _

corner _ _ _ _ _ _

Write '**edge**', '**face**' or '**corner**'.

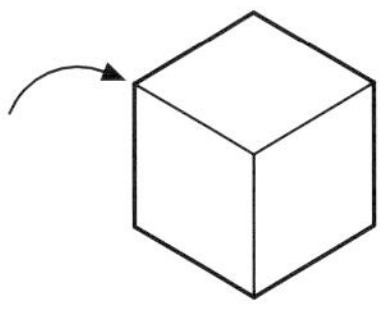

______

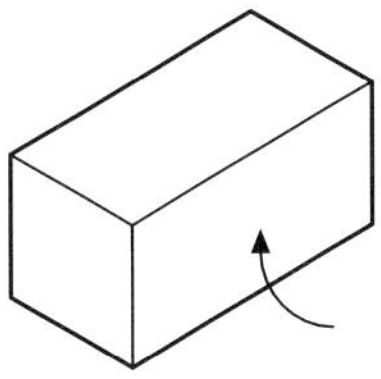

______

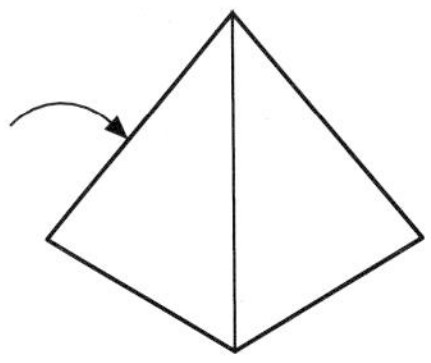

______

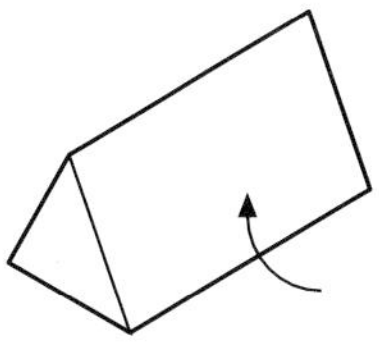

______

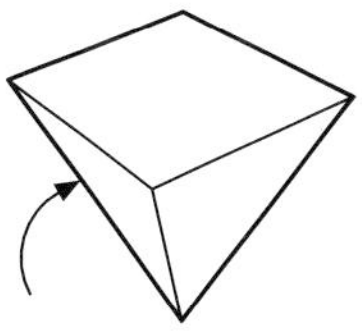

______

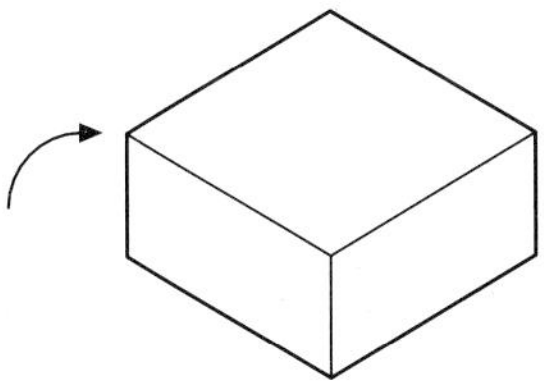

______

Name: ....

33

side _ _ _ _

Write the number of **sides** for each shape.

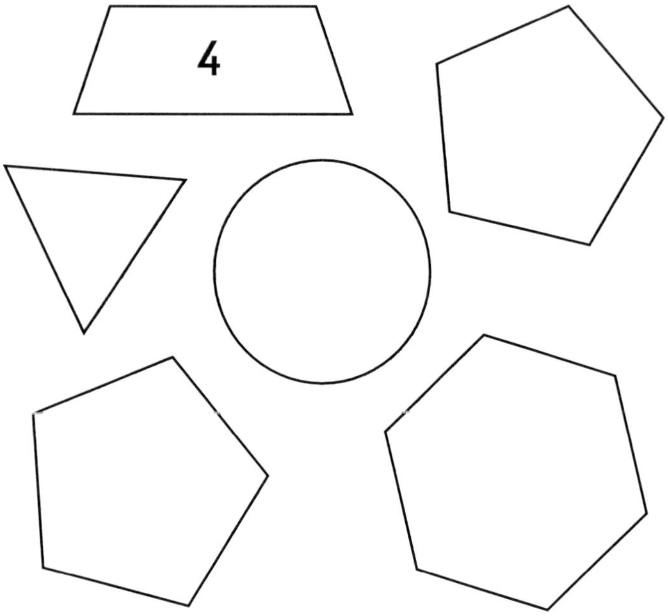

Draw a shape with 4 **sides**.

Name: ....

34

corner _ _ _ _ _ _

Write the number of **corners** for each shape.

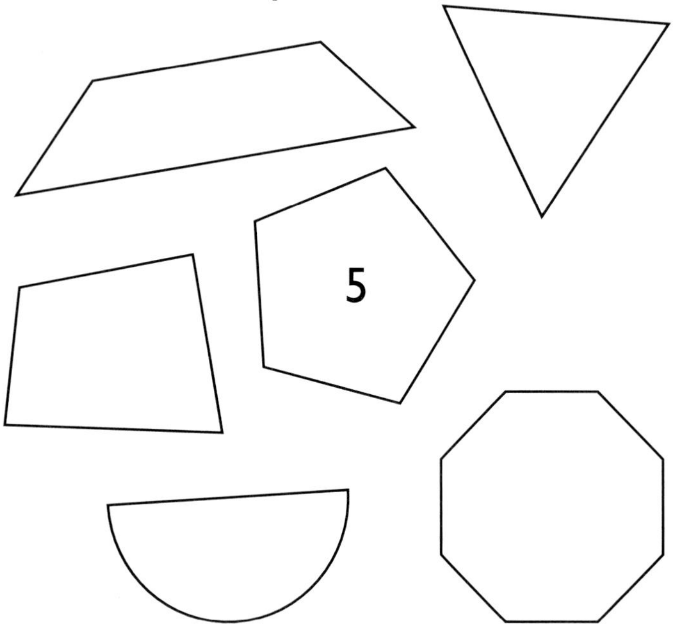

Draw a shape with 5 **corners**.

circle _ _ _ _ _ _

Colour the **circles** yellow.

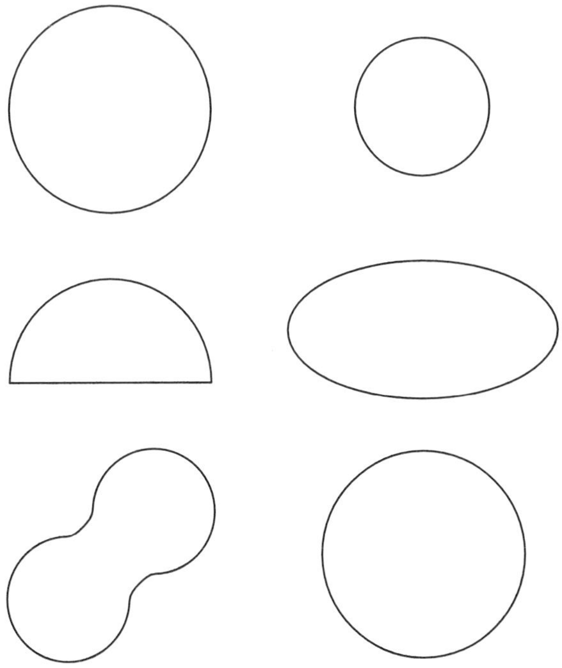

Draw a **circle**.

triangle _ _ _ _ _ _ _ _

Colour the **triangles** green.

Draw a **triangle**.

square _ _ _ _ _ _

Colour the **squares** yellow.

Draw two **squares**.

rectangle _ _ _ _ _ _ _ _ _

Colour the **rectangles** green.

Draw two **rectangles**.

Name: 39

pentagon _ _ _ _ _ _ _ _ _ _

Colour the **pentagons** blue.

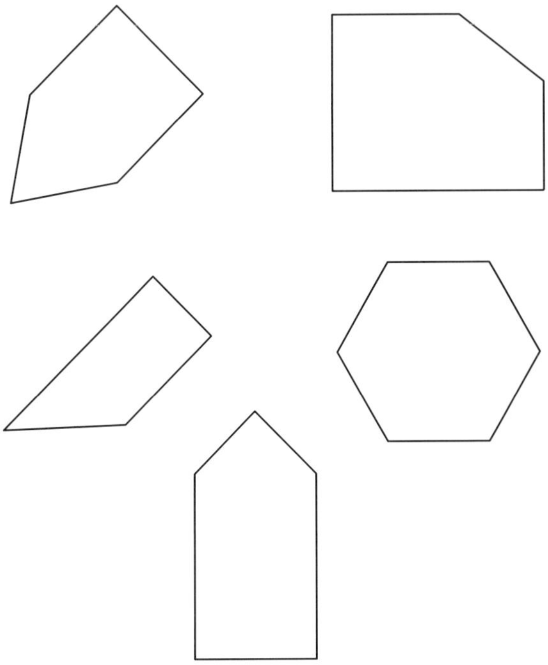

Draw a **pentagon**.

- -

Name: 40

hexagon _ _ _ _ _ _ _ _ _

Colour the **hexagons** red.

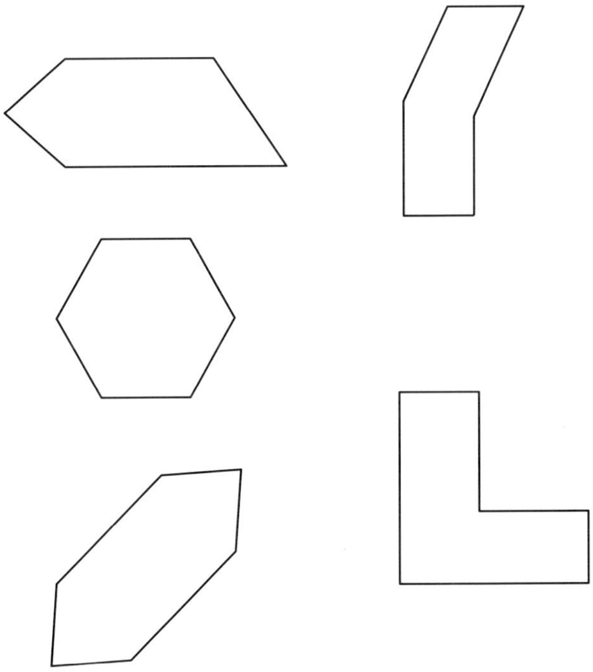

Join the dots to draw a **hexagon**.

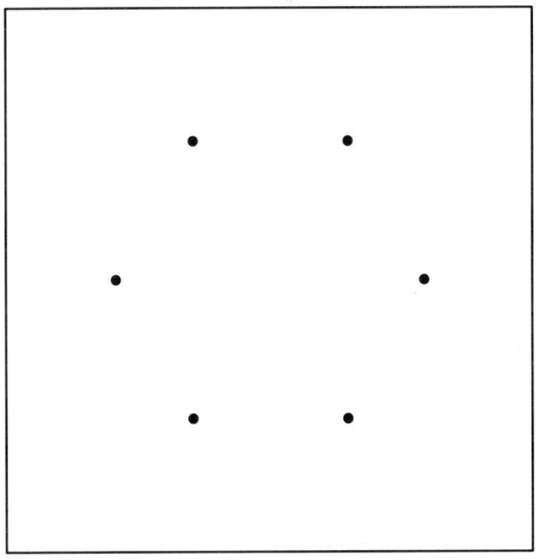

flat shape names

Join each shape to its name.

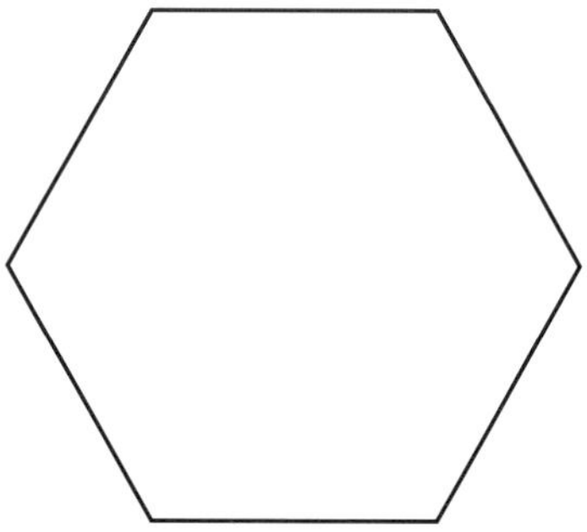
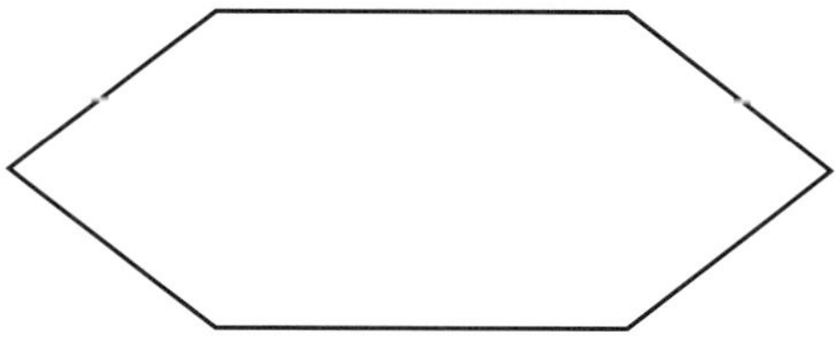
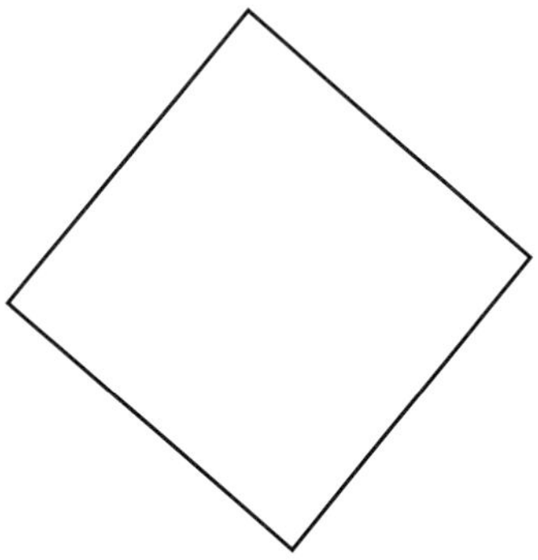
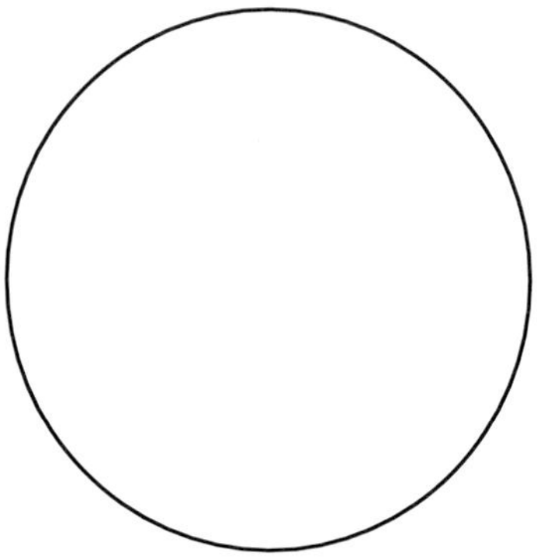
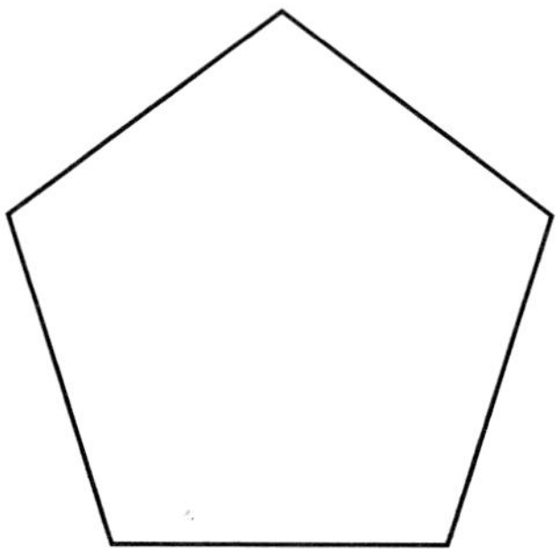

square

triangle

rectangle

circle

pentagon

hexagon

octagon

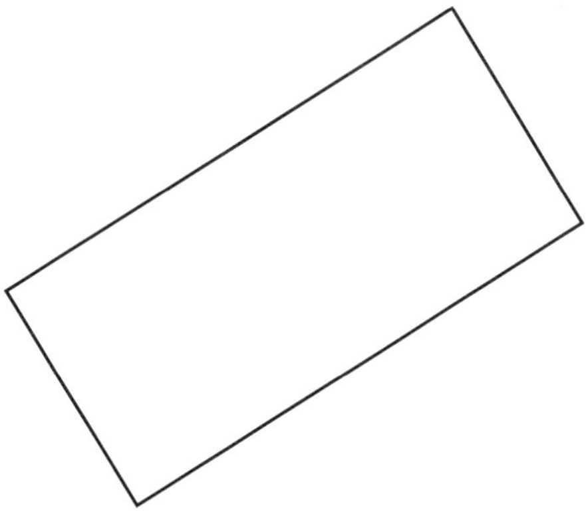
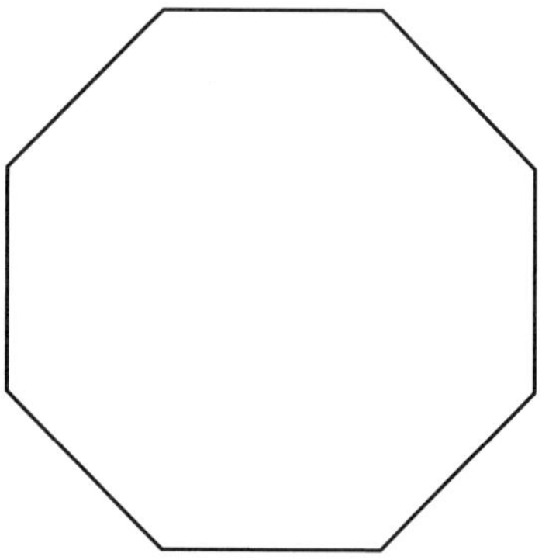
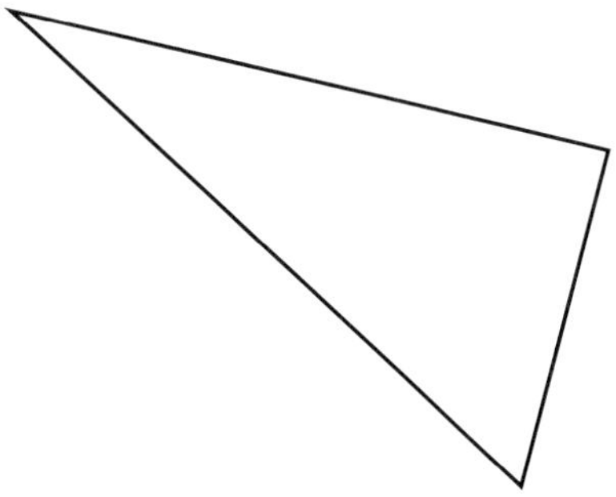

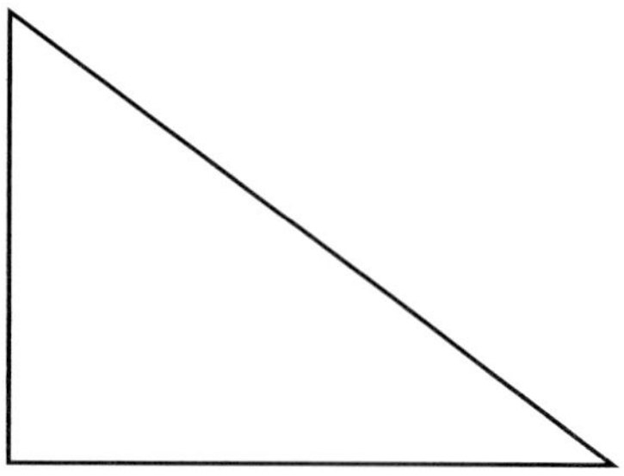

Name: ....

solid shape names

Join each shape to its name.

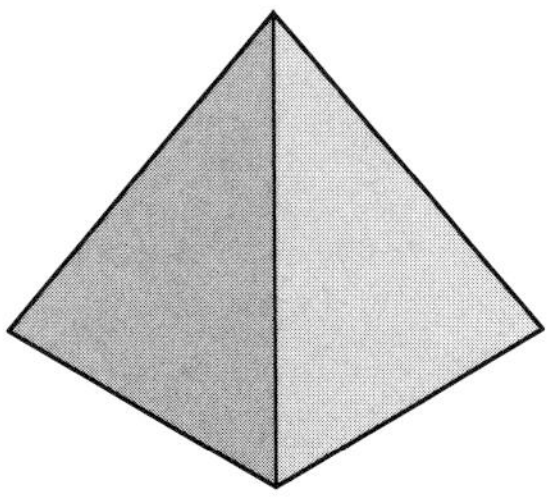

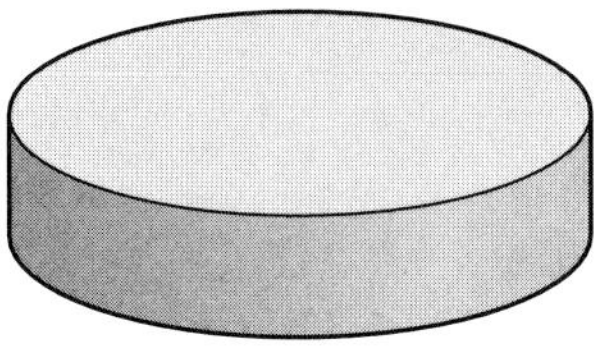

cube

_ _ _ _

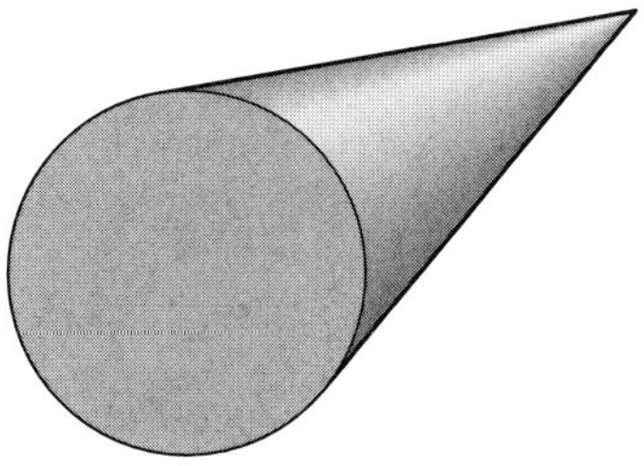

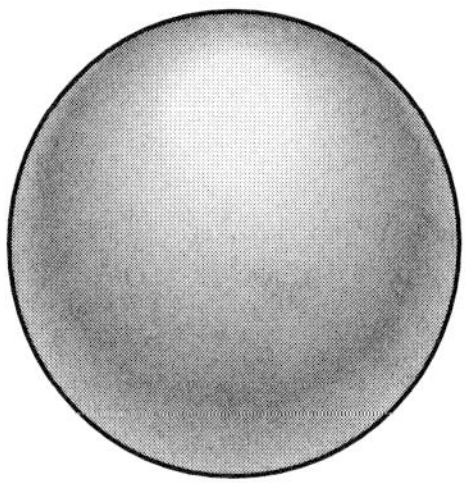

cuboid

_ _ _ _ _ _

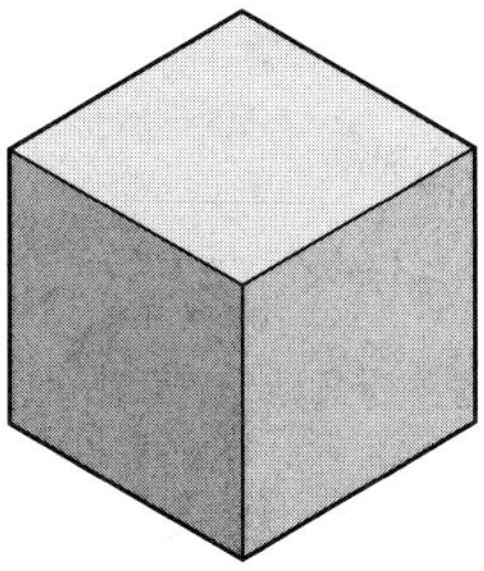

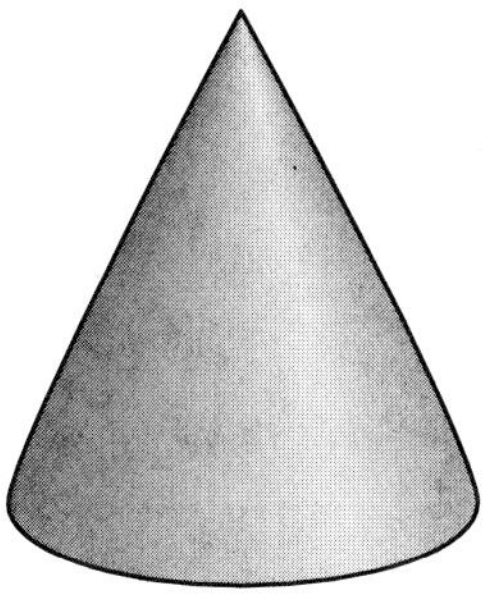

pyramid

_ _ _ _ _ _ _

cone

_ _ _ _

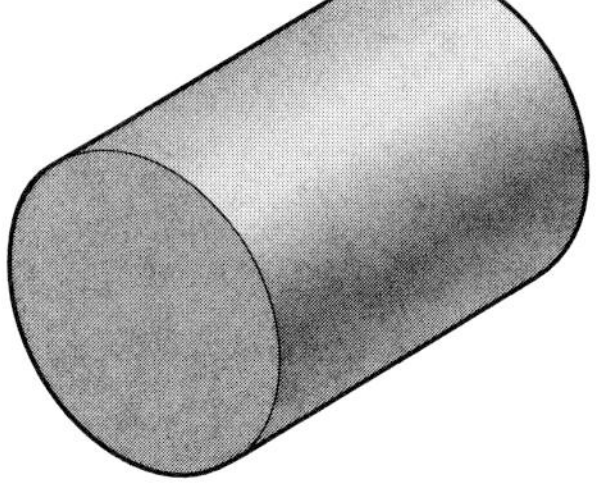

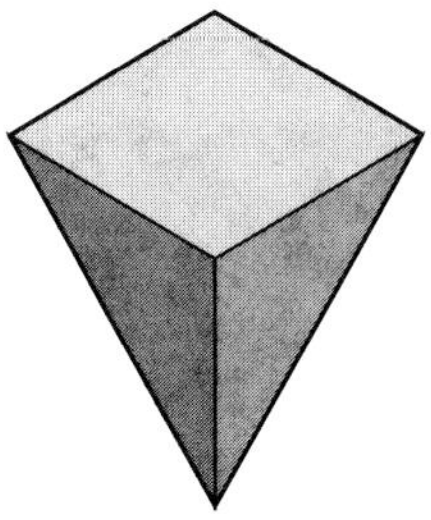

cylinder

_ _ _ _ _ _ _ _

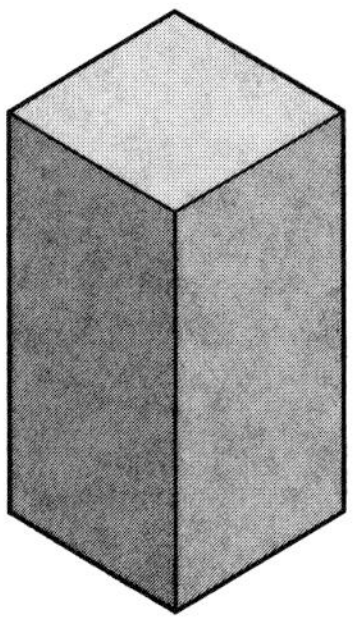

sphere

_ _ _ _ _ _

Name: **43**

symmetry _ _ _ _ _ _ _ _

Complete the picture on the other side of the line of **symmetry**.

Name: **44**

right angle _ _ _ _ _   _ _ _ _ _

Tick the **right angle** turns.

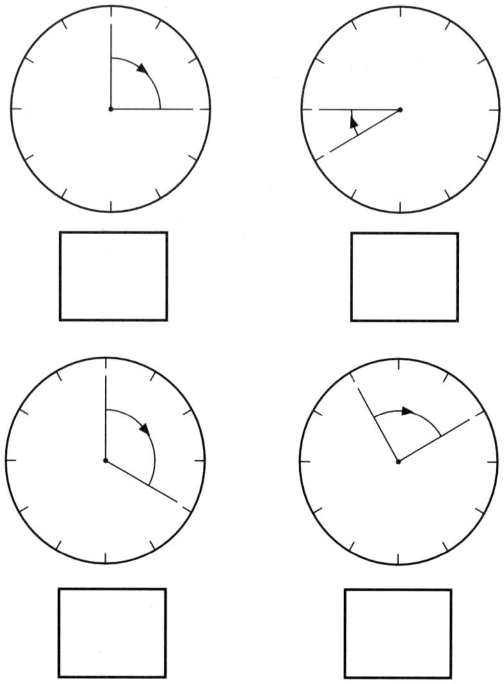

Write 'more' or 'less' than a **right angle** for the others.

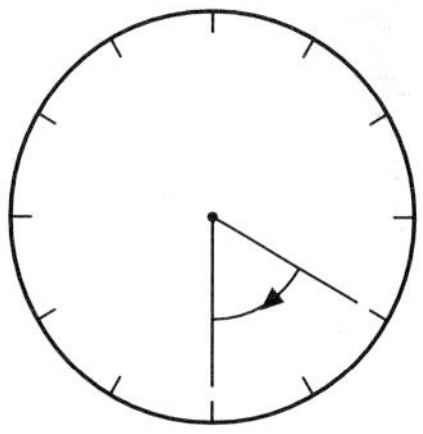 ____________

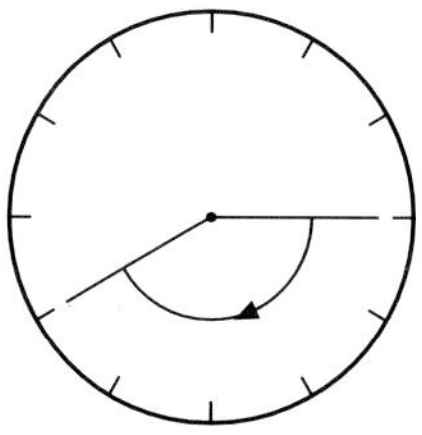 ____________